Great Escapes

THE CHESHIRE PRIZE FOR LITERATURE ANTHOLOGIES

Prize Flights: Stories from the Cheshire Prize for Literature 2003; edited by Ashley Chantler

Life Lines: Poems from the Cheshire Prize for Literature 2004; edited by Ashley Chantler

Word Weaving: Stories and Poems for Children from the Cheshire Prize for Literature 2005; edited by Jaki Brien

Edge Words: Stories from the Cheshire Prize for Literature 2006; edited by Peter Blair

Elements: Poems from the Cheshire Prize for Literature 2007; edited by Peter Blair

Wordscapes: Stories and Poems for Children from the Cheshire Prize for Literature 2008; edited by Jaki Brien

Zoo: Short Stories from the Cheshire Prize for Literature 2009; edited by Emma L. E. Rees

Still Life: Poetry from the Cheshire Prize for Literature 2010; edited by Emma L. E. Rees

Wordlife: Stories and Poems for Children from the Cheshire Prize for Literature 2011; edited by Jaki Brien

Lost and Found: Short Stories from the Cheshire Prize for Literature 2012; edited by Emma L. E. Rees

Great Escapes

Poetry from the Cheshire Prize for Literature 2013

Edited by Emma L. E. Rees

University of Chester Press

First published 2014
by the University of Chester Press
Parkgate Road
Chester CH1 4BJ

Printed and bound in the UK by the
LIS Print Unit
University of Chester
Cover designed by the LIS Graphics Team
University of Chester

Foreword and Editorial Material
© University of Chester, 2014
Poems
© the respective authors, 2014

All Rights Reserved
No part of this publication may be reproduced, stored in
a retrieval system or transmitted in any form or by any
means without the prior permission of the copyright
owner, other than as permitted by UK copyright
legislation or under the terms and conditions of a
recognised copyright licensing scheme

A catalogue record of this book is available
from the British Library

ISBN 978-1-908258-21-2

For Rosa, Mitzi, Dolfi, and Pauli

CONTENTS

The Contributors	xi
Foreword	xxii
The Elvis Shed *Philip Williams*	1
Western Isles *Clive McWilliam*	3
This Woman *Nicola Daly*	4
Monkshaven *Edwin Stockdale*	5
The Geologist's iPad *Tonia Bevins*	7
Delamere *Tonia Bevins*	8
Patti Plays the Parsonage *Sharon Marshall*	9
My Old Man *Simon Kensdale*	10
All the Days She Can Spare *Russell Morris*	12

Great Escapes

Advent *Suzanne Iuppa*	14
Her Hands *Suzanne Iuppa*	15
A Gathering *Caroline Jones*	16
The Pall-Bearer *Caroline Jones*	17
A Chord of Echoes *Gillian Wallace*	18
Tattoo *John Paul Davies*	20
The Innocence of Girls *Margaret Hodgson*	22
Shakespeare's Starlings *Sharon Marshall*	23
Weaver Cormorant *P. J. Beswick*	25
Angels The Swallow (*Hirundo rustica*) *Peter Branson*	26
Opposing P.O.V. *Simon Kensdale*	27

Contents

Confinement *Richard Rintoul*	28
Search *Philip Watts*	29
jam *Stephen Wrigley*	30
Seed-Time *Angela Topping*	31
The Orpington Miracle *Simon Gotts*	32
Front Door *John Paul Davies*	35
Hospital at Camp Bastion, Helmand Province *Don Nixon*	37
Luxor *Philip Williams*	38
Elements Beginning with C *Gill McEvoy*	39
Half-Truths about Cats and Dogs *James Phillips*	40
Longshore Drift *Olivia Walwyn*	42

Great Escapes

Sandsurfing on Hoylake Beach   45
Nikki Bennett

Three Poets by Chagall   46
(all of them lying down)
Andrew Rudd

Hiroshige at Work   48
(Tokaido Road 14, Hara)
Andrew Rudd

THE CONTRIBUTORS

Nikki Bennett has six collections of poetry, two CDs, and poems in various magazines and anthologies including: *ARTEMISpoetry, Still Crazy, de facto, Hearing Voices Magazine, Magma Poetry, Aspire, Ravenglass, Roundyhouse, The Poetic Bond* and *The Book of Love and Loss* (edited by June Hall and R. V. Bailey). She has read at poetry groups and festivals in the UK, the USA and Europe. She is a great believer in poetry as both communication and therapy, particularly in highlighting women's issues and circumstances. Her collection *Love Shines Beyond Grief* was nominated for the Ted Hughes Award for New Poetry in 2010. Nikki is a member of The Poetry Society and The Society of Women Writers & Journalists and founded the *uni-verse* poetry group in Bath. Since moving to Wirral in 2011 she has been an active participant in and supporter of poetry events in Liverpool, Wirral and Chester; part of a team reading poetry in care homes; and she supports the work of Lapidus – The Writing for Wellbeing Organisation.

P. J. Beswick is a resident of Winsford in the heart of Cheshire and is a relative newcomer to poetry writing. His family roots are firmly set in Cheshire soil and much of his inspiration comes from walking its lanes and fields, which is where you are likely to find him, when he's not watching Winsford United struggle on.

Tonia Bevins was sandgrown in Blackpool but has lived in Cheshire for many years. After studying English & American Literature at the University of Manchester she worked in broadcasting, then as an ESOL teacher. Now she wonders how she ever found time to go to work at all. Some of her poems have made it into magazines and anthologies.

Great Escapes

She enjoys – and scares herself – performing in open mics. She belongs to Liverpool's Dead Good Poets Society and is a founder member of Vale Royal Writers Group in Northwich where she has a hand in organising their twice-yearly Wordfests at The Blue Cap, Sandiway.

Peter Branson's poetry has been published by journals in Britain, the USA, Canada, Ireland, Australia, New Zealand and South Africa, including *Acumen, Agenda, Ambit, Anon Poetry Magazine, Envoi, The London Magazine, The Warwick Review, Iota, The Frogmore Papers, The Interpreter's House, Poetry Nottingham International, SOUTH, The New Writer, Crannóg, THE SHOp, Rattle, The Raintown Review, The Columbia Review, Barnwood, Able Muse Review, Other Poetry* and *The North*. His first collection, *The Accidental Tourist*, was published in May 2008. A second e-collection was published at the beginning of 2013 by Caparison Press, for *The Recusant*. More recently, a pamphlet has been issued by 'Silkworms Ink'. He has won prizes and been placed in a number of competitions over recent years, including a 'highly commended' in the Petra Kenny International Writers' Circle Competition; first prizes in the Grace Dieu Poetry Prize and the Envoi International Poetry Competition; and a special commendation in the 2012 Wigtown Poetry Competition. His latest book, *Red Hill, Selected Poems, 2000-2012,* published by Lapwing Publications, Ireland, came out in May 2013.

Nicola Daly has had poetry published in *The Rialto*, *THE SHOp, Magma Poetry, The Red Wheelbarrow, The Interpreter's House, Other Poetry, Mslexia* and many other small press publications. Her poetry has also been published in *Southword*, run by the Munster Literary Society. Her short stories have been published in Honno Press anthologies,

Contributors

and 'The Man Mayo Forgot' was published in a collection about migration produced by the North West Arts council in 2005. She had a story called 'Many Confessions' published in *Notes from the Underground* in 2012; this magazine is distributed on the Tube and other London transport networks.

John Paul Davies, a southpaw scribbler and member of the Poised Pen (thepoisedpen.co.uk) since its humble post-war beginnings, now lives in County Meath, Ireland (where he is definitely NOT on the Witness Protection Programme). Stories and poems of John's have appeared in *The Fog Horn, The Pedestal Magazine, Smoke* (The Windows Project, Liverpool), *Still Life, The Interpreter's House, Rosebud, The Cannon's Mouth, Pseudopod* and *Interstellar Fiction*; and he was longlisted for the Penguin Ireland Short Story Competition 2013. A poem of his is displayed in his favourite Liverpool pub, the Ship & Mitre. John is equally drawn to Yeats, J. G. Ballard, Iain Banks, John Burnside and Tom Waits, and continues in his selfless mission to sup a Guinness in every pub in Ireland.

Simon Gotts is not the son of a fishmonger, but he was born in Orpington in the 1950s, a decade that reeked of old raincoats and damp coal. ('Smog', his other poem about this period, was included in the 2004 Cheshire Prize Anthology.) Other highlights from the 1950s included watching lemon meringue pie made by stirring a pill and a gelatine capsule together in a saucepan of milk, and waiting for the squish on washday as his mother wrung the breath out of the pillowcases with the mangle. Simon moved North to Chester many years ago in the hope of finding such practices still prevalent. He has now extended his search to North Wales.

Great Escapes

Margaret Hodgson's poem 'The Innocence of Girls' was written about a 1950s Cheshire childhood where she had the freedom to roam from breakfast to tea in the school holidays. It was an innocent time which, looking back now, seems unreal. She has written poems throughout her adult life but only recently entered them for competitions. In her 40s she was involved with helping homeless people. She ran a resettlement project in Manchester for a charity called Lifeshare, so had a busy life with little time to write. Now she lives in Cumbria with her 16-year-old son, retired and having the time to be poetic!

Suzanne Iuppa is a poet, community worker and filmmaker who lives in North Wales. Her poems have appeared in a variety of literary magazines both in the UK and in the US and she teaches creative writing workshops across Cheshire and North Wales. Her poetry series *On Track: Poems from Welsh Pilgrimage* (Alyn Books) was the subject of an American reading tour in 2013, and she is a welcoming member of Chester Writers.

Caroline Jones is a freelance writer and editor from Chester. She worked as a journalist in London for seven years across a range of magazine titles including *Elle*, *Kerrang!* and *Wired* before returning to postgraduate study. She has an MA in Creative Writing from the University of Chester and continues to work as a freelance journalist. In July 2013, Caroline established *MISO* magazine – a print-based magazine for creative writing students – to support and encourage emerging writers during the initial years post-graduation. She likes Japanese food, Calvin and Hobbes, chess, Los Angeles, tulips, and John Berryman.

Contributors

Simon Kensdale is a member of that threatened species, the local government officer. Despite over-exposure to committee report waffle and number-crunched drivel, he still generates ideas. His work is characterised by a rejection of adverbs, literary/classical allusions, iambic pentameters and rhyme. He tries to keep it simple, believing that poetry should be accessible to any bright, interested adolescent (a theory connected to an early painful professional experience as an English teacher). Animals appear in his work, as do specific individuals and a sense of improbability. Down the years, a few – too few! – of his pieces have been published in slim volumes but he did once win a competition. As well as poetry, he writes stories and, not knowing when he is beaten, has begun a novel. He lives in Chester, where he campaigns for the Odeon Arts Centre (Hooray) and against UKIP (Boo). His favourite colour is red.

Sharon Marshall, a Scouse Debbie Harry, is a Senior Tutor at Bolton Sixth Form College and the founder of the Sherlock Appreciation Society and ALBHGA POETS based at the college. Sharon also runs Rossie Writers in Rossendale. She is currently studying for an MA in Children's Literature at the University of Bolton and is starting a PhD in 2015, researching Shakespeare and picture books. As a poet, she is simply in love with the contours of the English Language and lives in a romantic whirlwind of Emily Brontë, Dylan Thomas and D. H. Lawrence. She loves Liverpool FC and considers Kenny Dalglish's goals pure poetry in motion and his celebratory smile the stuff of dreams.

Gill McEvoy is a 2012 Hawthornden Fellow. She has had two pamphlets published by Happenstance Press: *Uncertain Days* (2006), and *A Sample* (2008), and two full collections:

Great Escapes

The Plucking Shed (Cinnamon Press, 2010), and *Rise* (Cinnamon Press, 2013). A further pamphlet, *Philomela*, is forthcoming from Happenstance Press (2015). Gill runs several regular events in Chester including the popular Zest! nights; a poetry reading group; and The Poem Shed, a workshop group. She can't resist organising events in a quiet way, but every New Year her resolution is always to do less – she never succeeds! She knows life is shorter than we think, so she is busy using that time her husband used to say 'God made plenty of'!

Clive McWilliam's work has appeared in *PN Review*, *The Poetry Review*, *The Rialto* and *The Forward Book of Poetry*. Although he is not a particular fan of horses, a surprising number of his poems are about them. Clive has been runner-up in the National Poetry Competition, The Troubadour International, The Manchester Poetry Prize and Poetry London Competition. He is interested in art and likes walking. His family are genetically predisposed to *almost* buying a dog.

Russell Morris is a fine artist and poet living on the border of East Cheshire. His work seeks to place the visual and the written word in conversation, creating a chain of associations between the two. The theme of his current work, and also of the poem published here, evolved while caring for his Mother during her gradual decline through Alzheimer's disease. The drawings, prints and poems based on this experience were brought together in an exhibition at Chester Cathedral earlier this year.

Don Nixon began writing about ten years ago. He began writing short stories and later started writing poetry. He has won and been shortlisted for various competitions, and

Contributors

many of his stories and poems have been published in anthologies and magazines in the UK, North America and Italy. He won the International Poetry competition in Italy at Lake Orta Poetry on the Lake twice for poems in the formal category and has won the poetry award at the O'Bheal Cork Poetry festival. In 2013, two of his short stories were published in the anthology *Crime After Crime* (Bridge House Publishing) and he has had poetry and short stories published in previous University of Chester competition anthologies. Recently, two of his poems were published by Offa's Press in the anthology *Poetry of Shropshire*, and he has been invited to read at various festivals. Retired now, he finds writing an absorbing hobby and through it has met many interesting people and made many new good friends. Last year he wrote a Western Adventure novel, *Ransom*, for fun, and to his surprise it was accepted for publication. He has been asked to write a sequel, so for the moment poetry is giving way to Winchester Repeaters, salon girls and the Rio Grande.

James Phillips has lived in Wallasey all his life. He has taught, quite happily, in the same Cheshire comprehensive school for the last 14 years. James was delighted to win the Geoffrey Whitworth Trophy for the script of his short play about Charles and Mary Lamb in the 2013 All-England Theatre Festival. He would like it known that he is very fond of both dogs and cats.

Emma L. E. Rees (Editor, and Chair, Judging Panel) is Senior Lecturer in English at the University of Chester and her specialist field is gender and representation. Her book, *The Vagina: A Literary and Cultural History*, was published by Bloomsbury in 2013 and will be out in paperback in the autumn of 2014. She has given her talk, 'Vulvanomics: How

Great Escapes

We Talk About Vaginas', many times, and in four countries, to date. She's also an occasional columnist for the *Times Higher*. *Great Escapes* is the fourth Cheshire Prize Anthology she's edited.

Richard Rintoul is a 21-year-old student currently pursuing an MA in Nineteenth-Century Literature and Culture at the University of Chester. When he's not face-deep in textbooks, he's slowly whittling away his existence in the retail industry, and listening to house music. His poem, 'Confinement', is based on his recent trip to a small zoo in the Jardin des Plantes in Paris, where he observed a Chinese leopard and multiple examples of the general public. He considers the latter species far more intimidating.

Andrew Rudd lives in Frodsham, Cheshire, and was Cheshire Poet Laureate in 2006. His poetry collections are *One Cloud Away from the Sky* (2007) and *Nowhere Else but Here* (2012). He is constantly amazed by the smallest things, and sometimes writes about them. He loves reading poetry to his 18-month-old grand-daughter. She loves it too!

Edwin Stockdale was born in Chester in 1985. In 2007 he graduated from Lancaster University with a BA Hons in Creative Writing and Music. Since then he has worked in a bookshop, a café, and as a nursery nurse and teaching assistant. In 2012 he completed his postgraduate teacher training at Liverpool Hope University. He now works as an Early Years Practitioner in a large community nursery just outside Chester. Poems have been widely published, including by the Brontë Society, Coffee-House Poetry, *Drey* (Red Squirrel Press), the Gaskell Society, *Ink Sweat & Tears*, *The Interpreter's House*, *Long Poem Magazine*, *Obsessed with Pipework*, *Orbis*, *Poetry Salzburg Review*, *Poetry Scotland* and

Contributors

Snakeskin. His debut pamphlet collection is forthcoming in autumn 2014 from Red Squirrel Press.

Angela Topping is widely published, with seven collections and three chapbooks. In 2013, she held a residency at Gladstone's Library in North Wales. Her work has been included in over 50 anthologies and many journals such as *The Poetry Review* and *The London Magazine*. After a career in secondary English teaching, she escaped back into the freelance poetry life. She collaborated with artist Maria Walker in a highly successful poetry and art exhibition which has been shown in several Cheshire galleries and most recently at the StAnza poetry festival in Scotland. Angela works as a poet-in-schools. One of her poems is set for 'A'-level.

Gillian Wallace has always told her writing group that she doesn't 'do poetry', but she's not going to be able to use that excuse any longer. She has lived with her husband in Congleton for eight years and it seems their nomadic life is over, though not soon enough, according to their children. Gillian confides that they did try forgetting to leave a forwarding address but the offspring were savvy enough to track them down! She's had a career of sorts in various forms of administration that taught her to use computers, and now she's retired. End of, as the grandchildren say. Not quite: she will continue to indulge her fascination for the English language, its idioms and quirks, if she can find enough time.

Olivia Walwyn is originally from Norfolk and now lives in Macclesfield, working as a school librarian. She has had poems published in *The Rialto*, *The North*, and *Ariadne's Thread*. She also enjoys fell-running and walking.

Great Escapes

Philip Watts was born in Sale, then part of Cheshire, read English and Education at Balliol College Oxford and, after teaching English in London for half of his life, returned to his native county 12 years ago where he followed a portfolio career including teaching, tutoring, acting as Interpreter Guide at Tatton Park, and working in his local library and a garden centre. He is now happily retired and living in Holmes Chapel, where he tends his house and garden, entertains friends, and writes. He has read his work at many events in Manchester and Cheshire, including Manchester Pride, the Manchester Poetry Festival and the Knutsford Literature Festival, and for several years ran OutWrite, a Manchester-based writing group which supported the LGBT community.

Philip Williams has lived in the county for seven years, avoiding the arrow that allegedly awaits unwary Welshmen in Chester after dark. He grew up in South Wales and attended a 'bog-standard comprehensive' which welcomed Gillian Clarke, Dannie Abse and other poets to small but enthusiastic readings. He spent two years in Australia as a '£10 Pom' and 27 years in Yorkshire where he first started to write poetry. He studied at Leeds University and has largely worked in marketing and publicity. He currently works freelance in marketing, market research and communications, predominantly in the education sector. His poems have appeared in *Agenda*, *Iota*, *Planet* and various regional anthologies. He hosts a regular Poems & Pints event in Alsager and is involved with the Poetry Society Stanza which meets at The Leopard in Burslem. He edits their blog. He's married, has two long-suffering teenage daughters and a twin brother who is something of a performance poet. They do talk tidy, aye.

Contributors

Stephen Wrigley is, after various successes and otherwise since moving south from Wirral, evolving into a Parish mag poet and raised veg bed gardener. His love of the countryside continues as well as for cake and ale, marmalade, sonnets, his family.

FOREWORD

The 2013 High Sheriff's Cheshire Prize for Literature was special because it marked the tenth anniversary of the Award. In 2003, John Richards, the then High Sheriff of Cheshire, approached the University of Chester to discuss the establishment of a competition open to writers with a connection to the county. With the unfailing financial support of MBNA (represented at the 2013 awards evening by Amanda White), the Cheshire Prize quickly grew to become one of the foremost competitions in the area, nurturing new and existing writers. Three previous winners were in attendance at the 2013 event: Clare Dudman (the very first winner, and author of *Wegener's Jigsaw*), David Whitley (author of the *Midnight Charter* trilogy), and Simon Gotts (whose poem 'The Orpington Miracle' features in this anthology). The Prize, which operates on a triennial cycle: short stories, poetry, and children's literature, is one of a very few free-to-enter literary competitions in the entire country. Indeed, Sarah Hilary (aka Sarah Frost Mellor), winner of the 2012 Prize with her short story, 'Udumbara in Lytham St Anne's' has commented that she would not have been able to enter had the competition not been free. Sarah's phenomenally successful debut novel, *Someone Else's Skin*, has just been published by Hodder in the UK and Penguin in the US.

There were 224 entrants to the 2013 competition, some of them submitting more than one poem, and 26 poets have made it through to publication in this anthology. The topics that provided the raw material for the poets were strikingly diverse. As in previous years, there was a fascination with memory and childhood, but butterflies and birds seemed to be the most popular topics: in these pages we have Emperor butterflies; cormorants; starlings, and swallows.

Foreword

Geographically, the poems take us from Hoylake to Delamere; and from the Congo to Egypt, Japan and beyond.

Deciding who should win a competition is never easy, so I'm immensely grateful to my co-judges, the award-wining poet Dr William Stephenson, and, from beyond the University, John Scrivener. The assistance of these colleagues also proved vital: Derek Alsop, Peter Blair, Ashley Chantler, Matt Davies, Melissa Fegan, Sarah Heaton, Frank Herrmann, Clara Neary, Ian Seed, Alan Wall, Chris Walsh, Sally West, and Richard E. Wilson. The guest speaker at the Awards evening was Roger McGough, president of the prestigious Poetry Society, who was awarded an OBE in 1997, the Freedom of the City of Liverpool in 2001, and a CBE for Services to Literature in 2004. Along with Adrian Henri and Brian Patten, Roger was a distinctive voice of 'The Mersey Sound' in the 1960s. The Poet Laureate, Carol Ann Duffy, has called Roger 'the patron saint of poetry', and I'm most grateful to Roger for his good humour and generosity, and to the High Sheriff, Mr Martin Beaumont, who made a presentation to each prizewinning poet.

The judges felt that five poems were exceptionally good. The overall winner of the 2013 Prize was the richly allusive and freshly inventive 'Elvis Shed' by Philip Williams. There were two runners up, Tonia Bevins for 'The Geologist's iPad', and Clive McWilliam for his poem 'Western Isles'. Additionally, the judges wanted to commend highly Russell Morris's achingly moving 'All the Days She Can Spare', and Andrew Rudd's deftly imaginative 'Hiroshige at Work'. None of this – the Prize, the Awards evening, the Anthology – could have happened without the behind-the-scenes, positively Stakhanovite efforts of the University of Chester's Corporate Communications team, especially Jayne Dodgson and Jenni

Great Escapes

Westcott. Dr Sarah Griffiths, of the University of Chester Press, continues to be the most patient, diplomatic and altogether serene general editor with whom I've ever worked.

A working trip to Vienna late in April 2014 was where the bulk of the final work on this anthology was done. The name *Great Escapes* had previously 'felt' right for this collection for two compelling reasons. The first is that the year of publication of this anthology, 2014, marks the 70th anniversary of *The* 'Great Escape', when 76 prisoners of war famously tunnelled their way out of the German camp Stalag Luft III. Of those 76, 73 were recaptured, and 50 of them were executed by firing squad. The second inspiration was that so many of the poems in *Great Escapes* celebrate or crystallise moments of escape and escapism. 'The Elvis Shed', for example, epitomises how art can grant us a temporary release into a creative space crucially separate from the slog of everyday life. Other poems in the collection find escape routes in the springtime, in love, in the natural world, or, most poignantly, in death. But it was a serendipitous trip to Berggasse 19 in Vienna, Sigmund Freud's last permanent home before his death in London in 1939, that made the title make absolute sense to me. In Berggasse 19, a small, naïve, black and white painting shows the seven young Freuds – Sigmund, the oldest, and his baby brother and sisters: Alexander (10 years Sigmund's junior), Anna, Rosa, Mitzi, Dolfi and Pauli. Due to the intervention of wealthy and powerful friends, Sigmund was able to escape from Vienna before Hitler could make an example of him (a photograph in the house shows its front triumphantly draped in huge Nazi banners). Alexander, too, escaped, to Switzerland. But of the Freud sisters, only one, Anna, survived the war (she died in the mid '50s). The remaining four all perished in Nazi death camps

Foreword

(Auschwitz, Theresienstadt and Treblinka) early in the 1940s. For them, as for millions of others, there was no great escape.

Emma L. E. Rees
Chair, Judging Panel, and Editor, *Great Escapes*
Department of English
University of Chester
1st May 2014

Note on the *Great Escapes* cover:

We're very lucky at the University of Chester in having a top-notch graphic design team who always do their best to come up with images to satisfy whatever seemingly outrageous demands are made of them. The designer Matt Houghton put together this anthology's cover using two elements: a Rorschach-style inkblot (a staple psychoanalytical image), and an extract from a photograph of the decoratively etched windows at Berggasse 19. The inkblot 'says' whatever we want it to say, of course, but its butterfly-like design, imprisoned by, and yet able to transcend, the filigree detail of the window design, seemed to fit *Great Escapes* perfectly.

THE ELVIS SHED

Philip Williams

One night a month it shifts its shape
for those with eyes for quiffs and shades,
the mutton-chop sideburns of lycanthropes.

It draws us like elvers over silver fields
or salmon summoned birthwards
by the phases of the moon.

We clear a dream-space between the pallets,
string the tubs and trays of mint-chip, toffee,
top-line rum-and-raisin with lighted strips.

Behind their awning, the freezers snore
and hum; chrome scoops stacked and resting,
like silent castanets.

'One-two, one-two –' breath thrums an amp
alive and in they come, flared and booted
for the Vegas phase, or plainer drainpipe sneer.

Now the floor's all coloured pools and platform soles,
the alchemy begins. There are chest-wigs,
shoulder-pads, a cardboard tube cargo-culted

to a sax with bottle-top keys and poster paint,
a mouthpiece that will suckle, squeal and sing.
We are lost and find ourselves all shook up,

freed from marriage, mortgage, earlies, lates.
One by one and lonesome, caught in traps
or crying in chapel, each will close his eyes

behind his shades – he just can't help believing.
And each in turn will leave the building.
We'll close our eyes and leave the building.

WESTERN ISLES

Clive McWilliam

A horse dozes by the cottage, his rump to the door.
There's weeping inside and half-eaten suppers
of butter and spuds, and their skins
soaked in milk still wait for the dog.

A squall has left the island darkened;
a ferry comes in sideways across The Sound,
where a fisherman in his tarry boat
is hauling empty water.

The ferry and the sorrow
come together on the shore;
a wooden box in the hold
has the cried name on the lid.

The road, silky from the harbour
up to one big star, nudges the garden gate.
The horse leans forward,
grasses rustling; moon on his face.

THIS WOMAN

Nicola Daly

The moon pulls at her like a tide.
On these winter nights, her bones feel brittle
and her knees are sore from praying.

By day she leaves the cats with their backs to the fire.
She tries to forget about the house built on sand
and goes to light a candle at the feet of St Anthony.

She dreams of eels and believes she can feel a pair
of warm hands around her girth but they evaporate
when she wakes. She blames the goat tied up like a
    witch outside.

The women lay branches of Mountain Ash on her
    doorstep.
A man from Wicklow advises her to eat either salmon
    or hake.
Her mother makes her drink a pint of buttermilk
and as she does, she wonders if her salt-skin will ever
    feel quickening.

MONKSHAVEN

Edwin Stockdale

'She was going to choose her first cloak. […] Sylvia, with unconscious art, soon brought the conversation round to the fresh consideration of the respective merits of gray and scarlet.'
                    Elizabeth Gaskell, *Sylvia's Lovers* (1863)

Sylvia leaves the farm on the cliff,
on her way to market to sell butter and eggs.
The buildings, long and low,
crouch from biting wind.

        Come to a crop of red freestone.
        Black-faced sheep browse
        tufts of fine grass.
        Jaded bracken clings to soil.

        Cross a tract of peat
        watched by a brambling
        foraging for seeds,
        but there are none.

        Go down the long lane.
        Hop across the river
        choked with boulders;
        water eddies in unfathomed depths.

Sylvia ties up her otter-brown hair,
puts on a black felt hat trimmed
with a grouse's feather found on moorland,
straightens the blue worsted shawl.

       Walk into town,
       closely-packed houses below:
       tiled gables, red-peaked roofs.
       Stop at the old stone cross.

Later, wares sold,
Sylvia hangs her head,
steps demurely to the draper's
to choose her first cloak.

            Emerge onto the quay
            at the mouth of the river
            crowded with fishing vessels.
            Today the sea is restless.

    Shelducks fly over cliffs,
    blend with distant sky.
    A whaling ship tacks through the horizon
    on its way to Greenland.

THE GEOLOGIST'S iPAD

Tonia Bevins

When you produced your iPad
I thought of Hockney in his East Riding:
flatlands, woods and wolds made vivid, enchanted
as I'd never seen them before.
And that the device is not the thing at all
but what it can hold within aluminium and silica,
its chips and rare metals, liquid crystal
giving up the pristine essence of a blade of grass;
rock strata, dunes, savannah filling the screen
in the contraction/expansion between
your deft thumb and middle finger.

I remember that lightness of touch
as we hairpin down from the High Peak:
how you can read the lie of the land,
what goes on beneath its sleeping folds and furrows:
the changing courses of underground rivers;
the upthrust of mountains, the mineral lodes laid down,
the deep past seeming closer than imagined,
given the advance and retreat of glaciers.

DELAMERE

Tonia Bevins

Not long off the plane, your body still in the pull
of another time-zone, we set out for the hill fort,
the climb claggy underfoot after rain.

I lag, wrong-footed in sandals, make much
of stretching my eyes across the Cheshire Plain,
watch the darting, swooping martins, the froth
of creamy blossom drifting, the almost perceptible
velvetting of foxgloves, tender spears sheathed within.
And the slow assimilation of an old plough
as it buries itself in rich red earth.

You are so good for my late education!
Today our focus will be mainly on sandstone:
shallow seas, glaciers and sedimentation
spanning aeons of geological time.
Sandstone, crumbling like biscuit between our fingers.
All those hefty town halls and cathedrals.

PATTI PLAYS THE PARSONAGE

Sharon Marshall

On Friday 19 April 2013, singer-songwriter, poet and artist Patti Smith gave a special benefit performance in Haworth in support of the Brontë Parsonage Museum.

Haworth as the New Graceland
For here the princess of punk pays homage
To Emily B, not Elvis
Horses, not Heathcliff
Clatter down the cobbled stones
As new chords coil round old voices
Crouched low on the lips of Rock and Roll
Charlotte, restless for the world,
Anne, steadfast by the sea,
Emily, explicitly Emily and no other
Ferociously her brother's keeper
She breathes in Patti's ear:
'My words my own, they belong to me'.

MY OLD MAN

Simon Kensdale

There are many sound reasons
For wanting the skill to paint
an interior with still life.

I'd like to be able to frame
a glimpse I caught of him
pulling on his sock one morning –

doing it as it had to be done
devoid of any interest
in the day to follow –

a simple chore,
the first in a series
the long hours would weigh on him.

He sat on his bedroom chair,
tugging. I looked past him at
the single bed, the glass of water,

the half-drawn curtains,
the oriental rug on the floor.
I thought as I looked,

a man should not be alone
at his age, left in silence
to pull on his sock in the morning.

But it'd take a Dutch Master
to link his action to the light
and my thoughts – and then show the whole to you

exactly as it was.

ALL THE DAYS SHE CAN SPARE

Russell Morris

(*Lifeline: a drawing*)

It's the way you were left,
with one hand clenched
in a fierce and pitiful claw;
your anchor,
blood-slow, cursed
and hooked fast beneath a dead sea of pins –
while the other turns to tapping morse against my palm;
a code I've come to understand and translate line to line.

For each visit a fresh page
where my first few lines float upon the surface,
until you appear
to be mostly watching me
struggle to watch,
as you endure
a few more hours of my desperation.

(*For a time of lasts*)

Your last breath,
your unexpected tear,
the making of my last drawing,
and then with your eyes closed and arms folded;
I leave a few coins tucked inside your evening bag
for the crossing over,
before the last kiss
of a particular coldness.

(*Invitation*)

At least for tea,
would you come?
I'd meant to ask sooner,
before you left.
I have your good china,
the best set washed
and the silver pot for Sundays;
I've kept all of that
in case you might find a way
to set endlessness aside for a moment.

ADVENT

Suzanne Iuppa

It catches me out while I try to park the car —
The white sky there, like a blank piece of card
And the birds freewheeling on it.
They make and unmake themselves in a rough V:
A piece of braille I can't read, and can't hope to,
Or not from such a height. So I go
Into the school hall, and find my seat.

From a sea of tea towels secured with shoestrings
You peer out, my singular Joseph, cramping
An awestruck Mary, flushed in the press
Of your friends. Someone's given you
A plastic jar of sweets to hold. And it's these
Sweets that hold me — to the memory of
Last week's fete game: how many in the tub?
While I laboured to calculate coloured foil wrappers
You nonchalantly drifted off to the cakes… and

How else would we face our table each morning?
How else could I kneel down to draw your finger
To the right number, and watch
While you open the window on the everyday?

HER HANDS

Suzanne Iuppa

Her emerald and its square cut
could make a cathedral of her cupped touch,

each year sudsing a new crop
of fontanelles, and Florida oranges,

or signal-flare a rummy spread,
holding our dealt breath close to her chest
only to lay us out flat—

Nowadays her strategy is
to place them invisibly
but firmly on each of my shoulders: *go on.*

A GATHERING

Caroline Jones

Stripped of its skin
the apple rusts.
Bites uncover
its core –
a fine-bone cage
grasping teardrop pips.
I bury the seeds
in a blanket of earth,
so I can collect
apples born
by the future,
and cradle
in my palm, fruit
like a human heart.

THE PALL-BEARER

Caroline Jones

I lift the exoskeleton
by soft, scaled wings,
placing its tiny thorax
in my palm:
a road-side butterfly
parched by summer heat.

My folded fingers
a makeshift coffin,
I escort the Emperor
to the canal bridge.
With one breath,
it pirouettes to the water
as I dust its pigment
from my empty hand.

A CHORD OF ECHOES

Gillian Wallace

One take, one flash against the sunset behind
and he's Kodak-coloured into the family album.

He doesn't want to be there.
He's awkward as only boys his age are,
self-conscious, stroppy, not hiding it,
stampeding into the maturity he fights,
can't handle, until it catches him off guard.
He tries a smile. But mutiny draws down
his head like a turtle under seagull strike.

He's there to lead our eyes into forests,
chocolate hills and the lake beneath.
Galleon clouds marooned in the sky sea
throw echoes onto a mirror, secret-dark.

Over his left shoulder, beyond the pines,
pebble fields flatten into a ploughed
pewter estuary. Guinness-flecked foam
blinks in and out, up and down,
like wind-lifted feathers
from an old flock mattress.

Out in the Bristol Channel,
bird tours bed and breakfast on mud flats.
Geese gabble, beat up into travelling vees.
Sandpipers sprint, stop, stab for buried grubs.
Terns whirl dotted wheels and seek asylum.

Over his right shoulder, across the valley,
there's a levelled place, an explosion of
tree bodies, spread limbs untrunked.
Target rings accuse the dead heart,
a hellhole furnace so fierce
it left no hint of pilot error.

TATTOO

John Paul Davies

Nothing as obvious as the letting of blood
for these brothers by way of initiation,
wrists crossed as the warm wetness seeped
into Swiss Army Knife rust.
Instead, a ragged blue circle stabbed
into the back of each boy's hand,
held steady to deter any act of cowardice.
Doubtful, the ten-year-old tattooist
had reached the top of his trade;
needle made white-hot in the corporation yard
bonfire, pot of ink pocketed from class.
Whichever one of them stepped up first
to prove this wasn't a game,
stomaching agony as the needle
snaketoothed into skin, the soft gristle,
ink floundering in the bloodstream;
took this solemn ceremony as the end
of time passing. In simple design, the blue spot
the start of a new understanding.

Forty-five years on, we have brought you back
to the Birkenhead street names of your stories.
Passing the corporation yard's spilt blood and ink,
the ritual site buried beneath new homes;
gone voices rising through the floorboards.
In this makeshift chapel,
as if to show off the tattoo,
they have placed your hands
one over the other,
which I now smother in my own and rub

that they should not be so cold.
Rub the spot as you must have done
when a new wound,
determined not to cry.
It's not so bad after a while, you said
to the others still waiting in line;
already tending the backs of their hands,
where the blue spot would begin to travel
as the flesh grew.

THE INNOCENCE OF GIRLS

Margaret Hodgson

Once upon a time girls played house
on wild canal banks, under tunnels of hawthorn.
Among lush grasses at the lip of the water,
dabbling their feet between marigolds and mud.
Cooling their heads under ancient stone bridges,
the buzz of insects doing the same.

Once upon a time girls played house
set out their plates of sorrel and dock,
picked a wild posy for a jam-jar vase.
Bluebell stems crowding for space.

Once upon a time girls played house
away from their brothers, hidden from boys.
Wearing their best daisy-chained crowns,
on long summer days drowsy with heat.

Once upon a time when girls played house
wearing trodden-down shoes forgotten by mother
across the meadows buttery with pollen,
wearing a veil of stiff curtained lace dusty with age.
Girls could lie fallow, away from the world.

SHAKESPEARE'S STARLINGS

Sharon Marshall

'I'll have a starling shall be taught to speak
Nothing but "Mortimer".'
William Shakespeare, 1 *Henry IV*.

Dark wave of menace shrouds the sunlight
Like Hundreds & Thousands wildly scattered
Sky bound aerial acrobats
Black arrows dive bombing
Breach traffic lights mock hidden lenses
Dart left then right cut strips of sky
Spitfire plumage switchblade flick knives

High wire dancing trapeze flung
Into netless skies catching throwing
Tossing wing flips and tips primed
Windblown flicking targets
Beak-pecked clouds speckled bruised
Playful perfectly formed shapes
Rise from nowhere chase tomcat prowlers
Flock rooftop rollercoasters

Trees dizzy shaken empty
Songs from snapping beaks leak loose
Their voices hollow nests abandoned
Feathered Harriers choke noisy traffic
Cloak human chaos caught by cameras
Stony faces set in angry queues
Lifeless statues stuck in dark jams
Watch these sky-jocks through jealous lenses

A symphony of clicks and whistles
A bird wave plunges 'Look! No hands!'
Flapping wildly ruffled violins
Little needles furiously threading tapestries
Before the slow black curtain falls
Spread-eagled dark molasses
Angels pushed off perches as pinpoint pilots
Pick through the eye of God
Pulling ripcords cut umbilical, and life?
Tongue-tied senses echo Tippi Hedren
A pale imitation like Baudrillard's wife

Clouds rattle on through open skyscapes
Yawn with salient semblance of silence while
Gate crasher sparrows scarper through fringed flights
And coil like Titania in swooping loops
Of aerial combat tempests full of sound and fury
    signifying
Flightless nothing.

WEAVER CORMORANT

P. J. Beswick

The cormorant applauds the river in ascent,
A late sound spent in a flare.
It settles into a ripple further on,
Its white grin wan in the lost light,
The serpent neck coiled
Beneath the foil of a beak.
Then slip more under its spell,
The grime of its back sits well in the moment,
The soot and shadows suit,
The way rooting to darkness,
And all the time the teasels' dry statues stain the air,
All that was fair, unfitting.

Sing as we go,
We touch the time and it slows within us.
The song saddens in the dark,
The ripple sealing into art.

ANGELS
The Swallow (*Hirundo rustica*)

Peter Branson

They move with speed and grace, charm insects on
the wing, style acrobats, the consummate
design, their sabre arms a stealth machine
re-jigging tousled sky. As ribbons dance
in zephyr hair, tail streamers draw the eye,
'scribe poetry on vellum blue. They bring
the summer off, sweet heaven's breath, woo heart
and home, twice blessed, so you're the willing host.
They brood in barn and shed, flash in and out
of mind, cracked slate or broken pane. Nests dry
stone wall, one winter's ravage easy fixed,
these will o' wisp, zigzags of doppel shade
and light, like careless skaters on thin ice,
kiss mirror images in shallow stills.

They slip the leash of everyday, possess
the guile to conjure four dimensions out
of three, one second here, but gone the next,
like wraiths. Their backs are dark-blue morning coat,
cream shirt below, the head and bib a bruised
blue-black, the throat an open wound, as though
by custom, rite of loving sacrifice,
the offspring suckle on their parents' blood.
They're off before you know, these semitones,
grace notes on telephone staves: it takes all sorts.
The old birds pass, their story told, like leaves
in grass, redundant punctuation marks,
last year's best clothes. The young ones hibernate,
the story goes, like bats, in hollow boles.

OPPOSING P.O.V.

Simon Kensdale

When the exhibition opened,
I overheard one critic say
The strength behind the technique
Was *'like welded iron bars'* –

The vigour the works *'contained'*
Was *'like some hungry lion,*
Pacing up and down'.

As if the circus had come to town
And we had to admire
The ringmaster's whipping style.

What the paintings said to me
Was that the artist, like a child,
Had somehow unlocked a cage
And then had stood back aghast,

Meeting those yellow eyes and
Breathing that foetid breath,
Before being brushed aside,

As a poor mangy brute rushed out
To hunt for the Africa
Lodged in a police bullet.

CONFINEMENT

Richard Rintoul

Each day they return,
painted beetles brought by a weak sun.
They cluster against chain link,
and a familiar drone rouses him
from a deep Congolese sleep,
hot and dark and spacious and green,
an African itch that twitches to life at night.
But he awakes to a cold grey day
and that old familiar rage ripples
beneath a coat of rosettes
as the gaudy things
squeal, mutter, gasp,
and the flashes begin.
His lips part,
flashing them back
the feral mask
they've been waiting for.

SEARCH

Philip Watts

There are seven in my area
Up for 'uncomplicated, no-strings fun' –
'Horny and ready for action';
Bi married professional,
With no photos on display
Except for one cock shot –
A sturdy phallus rising in priapic pride
From the flies of a navy suit.

And as I look at the balding businessman
On the platform, waiting for
The seven forty-five to Manchester,
I wonder if it's him, or part of him,
I've seen on my screen,
So impersonally personal,
Straining through the fabric
Trumpeting hidden desire.

jam

Stephen Wrigley

deep dark fruit
lush blackcurrants
sex in
pectin
bush tang
boiling
plush
as purple underwear
so scented
so seductive
on the tongue
I could
eat
you
all
up

SEED-TIME

Angela Topping

> 'Fair seed-time had my soul, and I grew up
> Foster'd alike by beauty and by fear.'
> William Wordsworth

Plants are resourceful. They try every method
to scatter their seed: dandelion parachutes,
sycamore wing nuts, jester's crowns of columbine,
poppy's wooden boxes that rattle like maracas,
rosebay willow herb's cotton graffiti everywhere.[1]

How unprepossessing the scattered seeds are:
black pepper specks, dried husks, pips hiding
in the apple's secret chambers, or buried in grapes,
sunflower seeds like moths' wings, schoolgirl plaits
of wheat ears, all herringbone and gold.
Strange packets of genetic coding, humble bundles:
instructions for oaks, copper beeches, aspens,
delphiniums, foxgloves, primroses or thyme.
Nurtured in soil's darkness, by leaf mould and decay
and worms' slow stomachs, by luck and skywater,

Winter's blankness proves them, until invisible threads
pull new shoots from earth, whether for a single summer
or a tree's long endurance. They take hold and flourish
on bombsites, verges, in fields, wherever they can thrive,
spreading their empires of greens and pinks and blues.

---

[1] The opening stanza refers to the genus of each plant named.

THE ORPINGTON MIRACLE

Simon Gotts

Goaded by the *Woman's Own*
curled tight in Mother's basket
I duck, squirm, burrow
through a spinney of support hose,
raw knees grubbing the sawdust,
inhaling damp gabardine,
till sprouting upright in the elbow-crook
of next-door's Mrs Sparrow, I see

the crab in black gauntlets
dressed to kill,
is dead as a kipper's eye;
scallops are nothing
but cold fried eggs
in Shell Oil shells,
cod roes loll
like sick tongues,
and how pitiful
the skate amputations,
(their sore red edges),
how deceitful King Lobster
held rampant on his plinth
by a rusty wire.

Over my head Mrs Sparrow
chirps brightly to Mrs Cray,
*She's got three
not yet at school
and another on the way,
there ought to be a law,*

*he'll kill her some day
the way he goes on.*

Nothing moves:
not the spoonful of pink sea
in the tray where
the herring tarnish,
not the Dover soles
stiff as table-tennis bats,
not the mussels
purging in their pail.
Only a child
would spy
the grape-eyed eel,
mouth ajar, tick,
tick, and flex his tail
as the current starts to run.

Tick
he senses the kiss
of the warm Sargasso
in the dried-up drain,
in our old rank river. Tick
he twists, rears,
thick as my bike tyres
stands erect,
slides from the slab,
shears the musty twilight
as their laddered legs part for him,
then blind down the alley
away from their shrieks
in a smear of bloody slime.

From the cold room
comes my father
in his apron
laughing, wiping his hands,
winks, pulls my hair
calls me His Little Man.
And bursting into tears
I know that I am.

FRONT DOOR

John Paul Davies

In the abandoned street
I draw the outline of the house in chalk,
pieced together from photographs
that survived the fire.

Along its imagined perimeter,
I find the room they brought me home to:
gas fire lit by a tear of newspaper
fed through plaster bricks,

steady flame in wet eyes –
my Father holds me delicately;
all the dreams he has for the boy
become tapestries on the living room walls.

I mark the spot with a zero
as the windows in the photograph begin to strain;
a refraction of light, glass shivers,
tarmac pours in.

Scouring the razed hollow of the back yard,
I circle the excavated beer bottle shard
that tore open my two-year-old knee,
etched this white-ribboned scar.

The gone house threatens something solid
as the rag and bone man's call
nears from the next street.

I step into the shadow of the house,
slowly receding into light.

HOSPITAL AT CAMP BASTION, HELMAND PROVINCE

Don Nixon

They screwed a metal plate inside his skull,
then stitched soft sutured tracery to hone
and smooth raw fissured skin stretched taut on bone.
His head is clamped so that he cannot pull
against this metal cage. I hear him moan.
and touch his hands, secured in plastic foam.
I wonder if he dreams that he is home
that in this limbo state he's not alone.
Held in this rigid iron mask, can he
remember? Is the past beyond recall,
like faint graffiti on a barracks wall?

LUXOR

Philip Williams

They have hooked out her memory,
drawn it punctured through her nostrils,
scoured the inside of her skull clean as a bowl.

They have washed her skin with wine,
removed her pith and stuffed her sides
with bags of natron to dry her like a fig.

After forty days they return with water,
resin, spells and paint. Anubis bends to tend
her, sniffs the salt and spices of the night.

Though forty she is twenty, voluptuous.
Before they bathe, wrap and bind
her close, they dress her as a maiden –

Then serve her all she needs: bread, fruit and beer,
shelve her essence in lidded jars,
leave her feather heart intact.

As the mourners smudge their cheeks
and seal their payment with their tears,
they part her lips so she can eat, drink, breathe.

ELEMENTS BEGINNING WITH C

Gill McEvoy

Carbon

forests
peat bogs

Calcium

ghost-stone
chalk dust
teeth

Cobalt

gleam of an eye
emptiness
of summer morning

Copper

red moon seen
through autumn leaves

Caesium

unspeakable

HALF-TRUTHS ABOUT CATS AND DOGS

James Phillips

I
Diagnosis
...of cancer via a cat rather than a C.A.T. scan

We like to sit and think
like Diogenes in the bath,
keeping a still vigil
until acceptance comes ... at last.

But red in pad and claw
cat palpates the abdomen
with inscrutable mien – no,
a Mephistophelean grin.

No need for scope or scan
the hurting relatives agree,
noting cat's submission
to metastatic ecstasy.

II
Confessions
... of a 'dangerous' dog's lead

I cannot tell a lie.
I mortify the flesh:
lash and lasso.

Dog lead for a bull breed;
an ergonomic bit of kit,
a necessary shackle.

Staunch, my links shine
still: not burnished gold
just Chinese steel.

I am what I am,
functional and cold;
the coarse leather loop forms

a neat knuckle duster.

And soon he'll clip me
to that gargoyle head

which jerks and swoons
when it relearns the breaking
strain I muster softens

its Doric neck, makes
its lavish fuchsia tongue
unfurl a little further.

Yet that rude-jointed cur
smirks, marks a course
its master could not charter …

Off the leash.

LONGSHORE DRIFT

Olivia Walwyn

This flow around the sun's
    warm bowl of beach
just stirred, sweeps
    us from its brim
our limbs
like pale fronds

twisting in the pull
    we turn to face
the spray
    and chop
the waves apart
beating a path

through the tide's
    course. Breathe right –
you'll have to time
    it for the rift
between one wave-lift
and the next, then fight

to rise. Breathe right,
    horizon sliding in a rush
towards your head
    churned light
breaks rough
you weave a thread

of silver, taut
    inside the weight
of water's drag
    displacing
down the coast. You're racing
and the waves

flip fast
    they're passing
with each pulse of tide
    each gulp of sky
and you, you're lithe
breathe right

you're slicker than a seal
    you're quick
you're stronger
    than you thought.
Strong as you feel,
perhaps you ought

to check. Breathe left.
    The pebble shelf.
Breathe left,
    and treading water
while you rock, spot
the little heap and bob

back level
    with the pile of clothes,
your shoes
    hugging the stones
like stranded bladderwrack
unmoved

look back
    towards the land. Between
your fingers grains of sand
    are spinning
onwards
in the waves.

SANDSURFING ON HOYLAKE BEACH

Nikki Bennett

The roaring reciprocity
of swirling winds
flinging their nets
in twirls, cross-hatching,
feather strokes,
mixes with smoky
darkness, misty moments,
near naked nanoseconds;

while the dots and dashes
fade into a faintness
pulled back by
a fierce force,
a searing surge of
adrenaline rush
and a salt tang
that stimulates, invigorates;

from earthy-solid base
aspiring to wispy lilac flumes,
and beyond, pulled by
plain sails of green and yellow –
our earth, our sun –
comes our power-trip, our sand-dream

pushing, pulling, piping us,
onwards, outwards, upwards.

THREE POETS BY CHAGALL
(all of them lying down)

Andrew Rudd

1

Three white birds
cavorting in the branches.

Lying here,
who needs a pen?

Poems, like red apples,
drop into my lap.

2

Thin poet.

Stretched out.

All the stable doors
open.

Saddle up your head.

Ride into dreams.

3

By the rackety clock
it's twenty to one.

A woman retreating:
they always do in poems.

Vertical floorboards are so
difficult.

You can't sleep
for being watched.

Or is it five past eight?

HIROSHIGE AT WORK
(Tokaido Road 14, Hara)

Andrew Rudd

A long diagonal scratch
into the wood: with this one line
the mountain asserts itself,
links heaven and earth. I flay
its flanks, in seconds creating
ancient gullies. I summon
black obsidian peaks, dot
trees into snow: each one
an account of centuries.
Off you go, crane. Now
you can stoop and forage
on my marsh of vertical
strokes. Now, madam,
adjust your hat, fuss
by the side of the road.
Day washes down into night.
I will choose colours
to dress you. I burnish
the paper, lift it from the block;
hold it to the light,
send you on your way.